C000231102

About the Author

Stephen Dixon is a well-known British broadcaster and journalist who has been on television in the UK since 1997.

A Cumbrian, he has remained true to his northern roots, despite having to move south for work. His passion for nature and quiet contemplation have led to this publication.

Love is the Beauty of the Soul

Michele

With lots of love

Stephen x

Stephen Dixon

Love is the Beauty of the Soul

Olympia Publishers

London

www.olympiapublishers.com
OLYMPIA PAPERBACK EDITION

A CIP catalogue record for this title is
available from the British Library.

ISBN: 978-1-84897-990-1

First Published in 2018

Olympia Publishers
60 Cannon Street
London
EC4N 6NP

Printed in Great Britain

Dedication

For Mum and Dad, Thomas and Isobel.

The love of a family crosses generations and never fades.

The Glory

Countless days of darkened skies
Are shattered, briefly, with surprise.
The shining sight of hope appeared,
Imagined, prayed for and revered.

But dare he trust its truth, its light?
To turn this ship round in the night,
To risk more years of shattered dreams
If this is not the hope it seems.

So faith is taken on its word
That glimmer followed like a bird
Yet on the instant, as in fright
It vanishes clear out of sight

And so he's left full of despair
Was it ever really there?
The hope, the love, a dream too much,
A glory he can never touch.

Bald Man

The woman lay alone in bed
She couldn't get to rest.
For fear of strange and balding men
Who could become a pest.

Why are you watching me? she thought
Why won't you go away?
Why do you hassle me at night,
And often through the day?

The bald man offered no reply,
He had no lies to tell.
He just stared longingly at her
And fell beneath her spell.

Beauty of the soul

Love is the beauty of the soul,
Soothing darkness comforts in the night.
The shelter that protects you from the cold,
As morning sunshine warms you in its light.

Calm is the centre of the storm,
Silence in the chaos of the wind.
Momentary sense of being home,
Stillness seeping into troubled mind.

Eyes are the truth you cannot hide,
The gentle whisper louder than a cry.
Perfection in a glance thrown from the side,
A look which says it all and cannot lie.

Love is the beauty of the soul,
Meekness is the strength that does not fade.
Caring for the ones who make you whole,
Sacrifice, the best way to be saved.

Bleak and Grey

I stare across the sea and see
Bleakness, grey and misery.

A fearful wind,
A fearful sky,
Cold makes nerve and sinew sigh.

Trepidation, endlessness appear
Amid the scene, so far from clear.
What lies beyond the vast horizon,
What distant land sees bright sun rising?

And why does man, with no real home,
Trust waves that rock and roll and moan,
To guide where none have gone before,
To find a new and sun drenched shore.

Final Meeting

I see him coming streets away,
Striding wide and draped in black.
I turn to greet him, say hello.
He's gone, brushed past me, won't look back,

Others try to run away,
Avoid his gaze at any cost,
Lives filled with dread of meeting him
What should be joyful years are lost.

I will not fear what can't be changed,
I will not lose my final grace.
Not shy away when my time comes
But smile and look death in the face.

Floating

To think of water,
To think of night,
The peaceful, graceful lack of light.
To lose control,
To give it up,
Be free and floating without stop.

Life has so many twists and turns,
Random callings, unseen warnings,
Impossible to find the brake
Until at last we fail to wake.

So breathe a little, take it in
The floating darkness majesty,
Where kith and kin or shame and sin
Are vanquished without travesty.

Friend

There are good friends and best friends
And then there is you.
Your black is my white
But your true is my true.

You see in straight lines
Whilst I peer round the curves,
You sing "Praise the Lord"
Whilst I query the verse.

You're strict and you're tough
And you tut tut tut tut.
Raising those eyebrows
When I start the smut.

I laugh and I joke
I tease and I sigh.
You giggle and wiggle
And sometimes you cry.

We smile and we sing
We work and we play.
We dream of the days
Where our cares are away.

We're a team you and I
The strongest, the best.
Together in harmony
Despite little rest.

We're not lovers, or others
Or useless apart.
But you always will have
A place in my heart.

And so my dear friend
I say only this.
I wish you all happiness
Forever in bliss.

Frosty Morning

The cold, bleak beauty of a frosty dawn,
The unseen night frozen in time.
To walk across a crunchy lawn
And see the spider's solid lines.
Each leaf a perfect work of art,
Each vein outlined in crystal white,
Beyond our vision to even start
Imagining all that lays in sight.
The gift of nature on display
In detail we don't often see,
Such wonder takes our breath away,
In clouds of mist so visibly.
But when the sunrise warms our face
And time again starts to move on,
The trees, the leaves, the webs all race
To change their beauty for the sun.
Such mornings are a special gift,
A peace and stillness in our soul,
That give our lives a needed lift
And warm us through, despite the cold.

Frustration

Frustration.
It's so..frustrating.
The pain and aching
Won't go away.

Why won't they listen
Or pay attention?
Am I alone
To not be mentioned?

I want to scream,
I need to shout,
To make them see that I exist,
To punch and punch with bloodied fist.

But then I stop
Breathe long and deep.
I need to rest
I need to sleep,
To take this stress away from life
To see it bringing pain and strife.

I am not wrong
I am no fool.
Ignore me
If you so choose,
But I'll not be driven by their sense
Of what is right, their ignorance.
Competing for imagined prize,
Using others to get their rise.
I will not play that selfish game
I will not clash and fight and blame
I'll be myself
For good or ill.
I'll clear my mind,
I'll find my still.

Goodbye

Stand,
Wave,
Smile goodbye
As loved ones board the cold grey train.
Tears well,
Breath deepens anxiously,
An unknown fear with that farewell.

Such pain is hard to bare,
Momentary torture of the soul.
The price of days of warmth and laughter
Must be paid in full.

It's not goodbye,
Or not for long.
Just a parting of the ways,
Reunited by a call in hours to come.

But the pain is real,
The tears are hot,
The wrench as raw it can be.
Take comfort though from love.

It's love that causes us to dread
Of never seeing that face again.
It's love that pulls our heart in two
As the train pulls out of sight.

It's love that makes us whole again
When it is time to reunite.

HOME

Feel the joy of being home,
The lakes, the fells, the trees like bone.
A thick brown carpet - fallen leaves,
That crunch with comfort, break with ease.

I stand on hillside - face the air,
The cold wind stings my cheeks so bare.
The bitter winter chills right through,
But my heart warms with golden hue.

Although I moved so far away,
Those distant country longings stay,
The thrills of city can't compete
With sight of mountain, smell of peat.

To stand alone in Lakeland range,
And see the fells that do not age,
Fills me with awe I can't destroy,
A part of me, as man and boy.

Inhuman

Mist in the mind,
Thoughts drowned in haze,
Sleepwalking through
The endless days.
Why can't I stir,
Why can't I mend?
This passive torture sees no end.

Relentless endless
Drug fuelled nights,
Where dreams are horrors
I crave for light.
But monsters ghouls and spectres show
Where in real life I cannot go.

So which is true the day, the night?
The gap between them disappears.
I know not which to dread the most
When should I feel the utmost fear?

And so I'm left inhuman now
A creature of the mind and soul.
My body lumbers, slumbers on,
Without it is when I am whole.

Isobel

My heart could burst from such pure love
A baby's eyes reach into my soul.
What will they see in her lifetime
And will she love me when I'm old?

I hold her in my arms and sway
To comfort her, to ease the tears
And kiss her gently on the face
With promise to help her through the years.

And now she calls me on the phone
With tales of joy and tales of woe,
And share with me the teenage angst
That causes yet more tears to flow.

She calls me uncle, calls me friend
I feel the joy fill me inside.
This clever, thoughtful, caring girl
Loves me – life is full of pride.

Nature's Kiss

I lie beneath a tree so green
Her branches stretch out far and wide.
The sky is thick and rich and grey
Birds sing warnings, start to hide.

They'll shelter from the wind and rain
Which nature tells them will come soon,
They sense it coming in the air,
A thunder filled spring afternoon.

As drops fall heavy from the skies
Refreshing all that lie beneath,
I close my eyes and open arms
A perfect moment on the heath.

I walk home soaked right to the skin,
But with a smile that signals bliss.
I've been at one with Mother Earth
I've felt the wet of nature's kiss.

Saints

If God exists what does she think
Of human kind, the human stink,
Of lows and lies and treachery
Of wars on land and wars at sea.
How can she bear the hurt and hate
Which in so many seems innate.
Why not destroy us one and all
And save this universe such turmoil.
Perhaps she sees some hope ahead
Perhaps a person born to lead,
Whose heart is light and full of love
Who will not judge us from above.
I think these people, human saints,
Walk among us day to day.
A friendly smile, a warm hello
To bring the sad an inner glow.
They won't be famous, they won't be rich,
They won't be worried about the glitch
That makes them weak and poor and meek
They'll focus on that inner streak
Of honest loving purity, of loving others, eternally.

Sweet Sax

Sweet, sweet saxophone,
Soft and rich and velvet gold,
Moving, soothing, wind me down
You ease my soul till I lose hold.

Worries, tensions melt away
As notes of honey wash me clean.
Nothing else is needed now
Except the smell of coffee bean.

With one sweet blow, my body writhes
A wailful cry that breaks my heart
Exquisite pain you can't explain,
The pleasure of imperfect art.

Oh sweet, sweet saxophone,
The ageless sound of times gone by.
You play your players, sing with their breath
Exhale a New York midnight cry.

Seasons

The Peaceful calm,
A soulful balm,
Sooths away the edge of pain,
Like standing in the springtime rain.

Joyful, light,
Blue skies and bright.
The flowers bloom sweet fragrance,
In summer meadows insects dance.

A beautiful serenity,
Gently washing over me,
Like fields of autumn morning mist,
A damp and chilled embracing bliss.

To be relaxed and be content,
Knowing that the year is spent.
The winter storms against the pane,
By fireside all is peace and calm.

Slumber

He lay slumped in a comfy chair,
Legs outstretched in candle light,
Eyes half shut - his mind half closed,
As music drifted through the night.

The window's arch was firmly shut,
As wind and rain blew at the glass.
The brick of old which formed the walls,
Were licked by flames as though at Mass.

Tranquility and gentle calm
Were warmly wrapped around his soul.
All tension, fear or heartfelt angst
Just eased away to do no harm.

Face shadowed by the dancing light,
He dozed in gold and red
Until he raised his weary eyes,
And slowly staggered into bed.

The Call

What is wrong and what is right,
How do we make that call?
Should we stand our ground and fight,
Or let our boundaries fall?

Our leaders tell us to believe,
They say that we must trust,
Ignore the call of our own hearts
And turn our hopes to dust.

Yet what of love, for dreams and friends,
The hopes we thought were true,
Should we ignore our souls' desire
And turn red passions blue?

We must have faith,
We must not fail
To do what feels so right,
Or else, whatever leaders say,
We will not sleep at night.

The Darkness

Why does the darkness interest me?
A deep despair I cannot see.

It melts into my soul at night,
But does not scare, it gives no fright.

It tempts me to examine life,
Why is there pain? Why is there strife?

Can wet, dark skies wrap calm and peace,
Round troubled souls that cannot sleep?

Will lunar skies ease confused minds,
And break the barriers of time?

What happened then – what is to come,
It matters not, without the sun.

The Last Goodbye

The time had come to say goodbye,
A last farewell to one so loved.
Filled with nerves, touched by fear,
Of seeing life in lifeless state.

A desperate need to witness truth,
To know she'd moved away.
The acknowledgement of life and death.
Brave hand holds coffin, but not dare brush her
face.

And yet it makes no sense at all,
It tells me that she's dead.
But is it her? She looks unreal.
A shell in which life was concealed.

She always felt so close by,
Just a call away.
Wrinkled lips keen to kiss
Firm hard contact filled with love,
That felt no need to speak its name.

But love was there - in waves and waves, anyway
you looked.
The weak tea waking 'Smiling Morn'
Apple pies and long lost tales.
The letters in her own weak hand, each word
etched with care,
Keen to tell she thought of me; the cat is well, the
garden blooms, a touch of home so far away.

And even in those final months, she feared not
what was to come,
"Time to be in the cemetery," said with no sadness,
no concern,
Just the tiredness that long life brings.
Ninety-one years of time spent well, content with
what's achieved,
"Shed no tears when I'm gone" my life has played
its course.
Yet tears they cannot be denied, but eased by
smiles and thanks and praise,
For closeness and love beyond the grave.

The Night

I stand outside and watch the sky,
The clouded night with orange hue,
I'm so alone, I know not why,
I long for love, I know not who.

The night brings peace, but sorrow still,
That life is lived alone,
And yet I must try to fulfill
My calling, which with birth was sown.

Others need my love and care,
And I must not withdraw
From giving all I have to share
To strangers, family, friends and more.

And so I watch the sky at night
Heart longing in the cold,
But hope still takes me, burning bright,
That one day I'll have hand to hold.

The Now

We dream of the future
We ponder the past
Beg each second to stretch and last.

Whatever we've done
Wherever we've been
It's never as beautiful
As it may seem.

So, we long to change
And rewrite our wrongs.
To sweeten the bitterness
Of time moving on.

But why can't we see
That now is the truth,
That nothing can alter
The dreams of our youth.
Whatever we've done
Whatever we've seen
The present is everything
Just be who you'll be.

The Real Me

It's in those eyes, those soft warm eyes,
That tell me who you are.
They cannot hide the thoughts you have,
They tell me that you care.
So blue and deep,
So clear and pure
The windows on your soul.
An insight into your true self,
A chance to see you whole.
And when those eyes are turned on me
You look that special way,
You see me as I really am,
It melts pretence away.

So, that is why I love you friend,
You see the real me
And fill my heart with hope and love,
You make me clearly see.

The Undertaker

The undertaker, tall and thin,
His evil eyes and evil chin.
Searching for the worst in life,
Living off our pain and strife.
He relishes in misery,
He smiles and rubs his hands in glee,
With crooked smile and soul so bad,
His day complete when we are sad.
Make no mistake, he does not deal
In death or anything so real,
The nickname earned in years gone by,
By making endless people sigh.

One day his tyranny will end,
He will not squash and crush and bend
The hopes of those who try to do
Their best for friends both old and new.

The grim mans life will come to pass
And after prayers and hymns and Mass
He'll meet his maker in the sky
Who'll look at him and just ask, "Why?"

Timmy

He looks at me with eyes that say
I understand, I feel your pain.
I'll comfort you with gentle touch
I'll kiss your cheek with tongue that's rough.

He looks at me with eyes that say
I need your love, your words that say
You'll always keep me safe and warm
And feed me lunchtimes, dusk and dawn

He looks at me with eyes that say
I can't be sure just what you are.
Trust you? Yes I'm sure I can,
But are you cat or are you man?

I look at him with eyes that say
Thank you friend, my love, my pal.
You bring such comfort, peace and joy
My pretty, purring, perfect boy.

To no avail

To try to try, to no avail,
Can hope survive when efforts fail?
The heart demands the fight goes on,
But strength is weak, all faith is gone.

I know what's right, I know what's wrong,
But when I shout there is no-one
Who'll listen to me, understand,
I'm left alone on no man's land.

Why do the others turn away
Why don't they stop, why don't they say
How can we change what's going on?
Why don't they stop what's going wrong.

So do I follow heart's desire
Fighting on and face the ire,
Or just give up and creep away
Losing the will to try to stay?

Watching

Thousands of people bustle by
Rushing past the window pane,
Meetings, greetings, always late,
Collars high against the rain.

The cafe seems so comforting,
The steaming tea, the slice of cake,
Ignoring the departure board
Relaxing in the others' wake.

Where will these people end their day?
What journeys long into the night?
A long-awaited friend to see
Or homeward bound to smiles so bright.

Such pleasure comes from sitting by
Pondering lives in mystery
A fleeting glance into a soul
Imagining things that may not be.

Home Town

Walking round the old home town
A secret past brought back to life,
A school, a church, an empty bar,
Form vivid thoughts of joy and strife.

Feel lost in a place you once belonged
Confuses heart and mind and soul,
Where would I be if I had stayed?
Would I be me – would I be whole?

Some say look only ever forward,
Forget the past, pay it no heed,
But facing back to see our pathway
Shows us how and why we bleed.

Sometimes we need the pain of history
Even good times bring regrets.
Those days can never be repeated,
We cannot walk in our old steps.

So while events in time do shape us,
Memories formed like works of art,
We are not forged alone by past life,
We are not just a sum of parts.

Mother

Mother, my mother
The bringer of life.
Sharer of joy
And a comfort in strife.

Your face is the image
Of love unsurpassed.
Your smile is so genuine
Nothing is masked.

My love for you feels so pure and so raw,
Nothing can bend it or break it or more.
Distance or time will not take you from me,
A son to my mother, eternally.

What Matters

A good job,
A great job
That makes you so rich.
Or fame and celebrity,
Being a bitch.
A boss with a scotch and cigar in his teeth
A councillor showing off his latest speech.
The matriarch always one up on the Joneses,
The silver, the olives, the dinners, the roses.
These people all desperate to be something else,
Worried they're left on history's shelf.
So lives are filled up with things that don't matter
Fake status, fake happiness, need people to chatter.
None of it counts at the end of day,
It's not real life, whatever they say.
Love is the only richness in life,
From friends and companions, husband or wife.
To know that you mean something to someone,
To know you'll be missed when your time is done.